Leeds Castle

MAIDSTONE · KENT

© 1994 Leeds Castle Foundation

First published 1989 on behalf
of Leeds Castle Foundation
by Philip Wilson Publishers Limited
143–149 Great Portland Street
London W1N 5FB

Revised edition 1994
Reprinted 1996

Designed by Mavis Henley

Printed in England by
BPC Magazines (Dunstable) Limited
on Fineblade Smooth paper
manufactured by Smurfit Townsend Hook Limited,
Snodland, Kent

*Changes may be made to the works of art,
furniture and other items on display in the public
rooms at the Castle which may be closed from
time to time without notice.*

Contents

Foreword   PAGE 4

The History of the Castle   PAGE 7

**The Park, Duckery, Wood Garden, Mill
and Barbican**   PAGE 29

The Castle Within   PAGE 35

**The Culpeper Garden, Aviary, Maze and Grotto,
Greenhouses and Vineyard**   PAGE 63

Leeds Castle Today   PAGE 73

Acknowledgements   PAGE 80

Raised on an island, Leeds Castle, oldest and most romantic of England's 'stately homes', was first built in stone by a Norman baron in the reign of William the Conqueror's son, Henry I, nearly 900 years ago. A century and a half later, on the accession of Edward I – the King whose adage that what concerns all should be approved by all, makes him, more than any other of our sovereigns, the real founder of our Parliament – this formidable baronial fortress, as it then was, came into the possession of the Crown. For the next three centuries a royal palace and the castle of six of England's medieval queens, it later passed, through royal grant and subsequent purchases, into the hands of three famous English families – the St Legers, the Culpepers and the Fairfaxes – until, in our own century, it was bought from its then owners, the Wykeham Martins, by Lady Baillie – daughter, by his American Whitney wife, of my old friend the late Almeric Paget, Lord Queenborough, whose grandfather commanded the British cavalry at Waterloo. It was Olive Baillie's lifelong love for, and devoted restoration of, this ancient and beautiful castle with its lovely park and gardens, together with her vision and generosity which, after a lapse of four centuries, brought about its re-dedication to the service of the nation.

It is strange how often the history of this romantic castle has impinged on the wider history of both England and America. The earliest of the queens whose loved home it was, was the Spanish princess Eleanor of Castile, who saved the life of her crusading husband after he was struck down by an assassin's poisoned dagger at Acre. Edward's love for this noble, stately woman, with her long, dark, Spanish tresses and calm Gothic features, proved the guiding star of his life, the happiest part of which was spent with her at Leeds Castle. 'My harp is turned to mourning,' he wrote after she died, 'in life I loved her dearly, nor can I cease to love her in death.' At every place where her bier rested on its journey to Westminster, he raised a cross in her memory, the name of the last of which, the *chère reine* (or Charing) cross, has survived in that of the London thoroughfare where Dr Johnson maintained that the full tide of human existence was best to be encountered.

FOREWORD

BY SIR ARTHUR BRYANT CH

The arms shown on this and the following page are those of Edward I and Eleanor of Castile, the first of England's queens to hold Leeds Castle.

Another royal romance associated with Leeds Castle was that of Queen Catherine de Valois – widow of Henry V and the 'French Kate' of Shakespeare's play – who, while living there, fell in love with and secretly married her Clerk of the Wardrobe, an obscure but handsome young Welsh squire named Owen Tudor. The offspring of this concealed and scandalous match, as it seemed to contemporaries, was the father of Henry Tudor, who, after his victory at Bosworth Field, became, as Henry VII, the founder of the greatest of all England's historic dynasties. It was at Leeds that the first Tudor's still more famous son, Henry VIII, enriched the Castle with its noble banqueting hall.

Froissart in his *Chronicles* recorded his attendance on King Richard II in his 'beautiful palace in Kent called Leeds Castle', which that tragic king afterwards gave to his child bride, Anne of Bohemia. Edward VIII, when Prince of Wales, was a guest here in the days of its last châtelaine, Lady Baillie; and, during the second world war, Field Marshal Montgomery and Sir Bertram Ramsay, the Admiral who commanded the Allied naval operations on D Day, were among those who came on their wartime business to this great towered haunt of ancient peace and 'battles long ago', still dreaming in its encircling lake.

Perhaps the most extraordinary of all the castle's historic associations is that with the United States. One of its owners, Sir Warham St Leger, was closely associated with Sir Walter Raleigh, the man whose lifelong dream – one for which he died on the scaffold – had been to found a new English nation on the far side of the Atlantic. During his starveling and perilous years of exile, Charles II rewarded one of his followers, Lord Culpeper, for his fidelity by a grant of more than five million acres of virgin American soil, so making him the 'Lord Proprietor' of what was to become the heartland of colonial North America. He and his immediate heirs were the greatest landowners known to American history. The last of them, the 6th Lord Fairfax – a relative of the victor of Marston Moor and Naseby – emigrated to America during the reign of George II, and was the friend and first employer of the young George Washington, who helped to survey part of his vast under-developed estates on the wild western Virginian frontier. After he had become the leader of an independent American nation, Washington praised 'the good old lord' who, living to the age of 89, carried on in the New World the traditions of generosity, liberality and good neighbourliness which he had learnt in youth at Leeds Castle.

Now the wheel of history has come full circle, and Lady Baillie, with the help of the inheritance from her American Whitney mother, has provided under her will that this wonderful Norman castle, whose former owner left it to follow his fortunes in the New World, is to be preserved in perpetuity for the public benefit as a centre of the arts, of charitable work and, in particular, for medical conferences in peaceful surroundings with the great physicians and scientists of all nations. No lovelier spot on earth could be found for such a purpose.

'Wonderful in manifold glories,' wrote the historian of castles, Lord Conway, 'are the great castle visions of Europe; Windsor from the Thames, Warwick or Ludlow from their riversides, Conway or Carnarvon from the sea, Amboise from the Loire, Aigues Mortes from the lagoons, Carcassonne, Coucy, Falaise and Château Gaillard – beautiful as they are and crowned with praise, are not comparable in beauty with Leeds, beheld among the waters on an autumnal evening when the bracken is golden and there is a faint blue mist among the trees – the loveliest castle, as thus beheld, in the whole world.'

The History of the Castle

From Saxon to Plantagenet

Leeds Castle, named after the nearby village of Leeds (Saxon Esledes), was originally a manor of the Saxon royal family possibly as early as the reign of Ethelbert IV (856–860). In the years immediately preceding the victorious Norman Conquest King Edward the Confessor granted the Manor to the powerful house of Godwin.

After the Conquest, the victorious Norman barons were surrounded and vastly outnumbered by the hostile English, so they subdued the conquered country by building strong castles. In 1090 William II *Rufus* granted the Manor of Leeds to his cousin, Hamo de Crèvecoeur, who had fought in the Conqueror's army at the Battle of Hastings.

Around 1119 Robert de Crèvecoeur started to build a stone castle on the site, establishing his *donjon* (keep or main fortification) where the Gloriette now is. As the castle stands beside the River Len, the mill, which predates the Domesday survey of 1086, was incorporated into the defences at the outer gates. Almost certainly a drawbridge connected the fortified mill to the inner gatehouse. What is now the largest island was surrounded by high walls of some 30 to 50 feet inside the revetment wall. Domestic buildings were located at the northern end of the bailey (walled area around the keep) and connected to the keep by a drawbridge over the water-filled ditch.

Following Henry I's death in 1135, Stephen, Count of Blois, and his cousin the Empress Matilda contested the crown of England. In 1139 Matilda invaded England with the help of her brother Robert, Earl of Gloucester, who held Leeds Castle, but Kent was loyal to King Stephen and following a short siege he took control of the castle.

Sir Robert de Crèvecoeur, great-great-grandson of the original builder of the castle, fought against Henry III at the Battle of Lewes (1264), and following the king's decisive victory at Evesham in 1265 his family's fortunes went into decline. Sir Robert de Crèvecoeur was obliged to yield Leeds Castle to Sir Roger de Leyburn, friend and supporter of Henry III, and it was his son William, 1st Lord Leyburn – also a great fighting baron high in the king's favour – who in 1278 conveyed Leeds Castle 'to the august prince and my most dear Lord Edward the noble King of England and my fair Lady Elinor Queen of England.'

At Leeds the third division of the castle is the barbican (outwork defending castle entrances). It is of unique construction, placed on the outer wall of the dam, at this point reduced to fifty feet in width. The barbican was composed of three parts, once isolated by wet ditches, and had three entrances, each with its own drawbridge, gateway and portcullis, one from each wing of the dam.

These approaches converged on a central plot, open towards the castle, at the bridge of two arches leading to the gatehouse. Originally the inner arch was open between the parapet for the pit of the drawbridge. At the south end of the barbican was a strongly fortified mill, ruined since the 1650s, through which an aqueduct, in its basement storey, conveyed water to flood the Len valley in time of danger. This triple composition for a barbican has not been found anywhere else.

The age of chivalry: the three Edwards

So began the long royal ownership of Leeds Castle, and it opened brilliantly because Edward I and his queen Eleanor of Castile, daughter of St Ferdinand III, King of Castile and Leon, both loved the castle, using it for rest and hunting. Through them also, the castle's links with the Continent were extended. Edward's mother was Eleanor of Provence and his own queen introduced continental refinements, such as carpets, to the English way of life.

Edward I carried out extensive alterations to the castle. Taking advantage of the site, his engineers perfected the embankments surrounding the moat, here a defensive lake, which in all probability dates from the closing years of the Crèvecoeur occupation. A large dam was constructed to hold in the waters not only of the lake but also of the Great Water which could be formed by flooding the valley of the Len in time of danger. To protect the dam a barbican of unusual design was constructed, connected to the mill and outer gatehouse. A revetment wall, rising sheer from the water, was built around the largest island. At intervals the wall was strengthened by D-shaped turrets which originally had upper storeys almost certainly loop-holed. The gatehouse was advanced to the edge of the revetment wall in order to afford greater protection to the dam and barbican. Its southern wall and arch can be seen just inside the main gateway. Within the enlarged gatehouse were the quarters of the Constable and castle guard. Beyond the barbican and mill the three approach roads were all across causeways, which gave added protection by reducing opportunities for attack. Domestic buildings stood at the northern end of the main island. Beyond these, drawbridges connected it to the keep, here called the Gloriette (a Spanish term for a pavilion at the intersection of a Moorish garden arising from Eleanor of Castile's influence). Its principal apartment was the hall occupying much of the west side. Edward I was careful in monetary matters and during his time the apartments, when occupied, though comfortable, would not have been luxurious.

In medieval times, marriage was regarded by kings and great barons almost entirely as a means of increasing or safeguarding their power and wealth. It was indeed to protect the southern boundary of his French possessions in Gascony that Edward had originally married Eleanor of Castile, but gradually he grew to love her deeply.

From the Itinerary of Edward I's reign it is known he and Queen Eleanor were in residence at Leeds Castle from 16 to 27 August 1289, after returning from an extended visit to their dominions in Gascony – indicating one of the castle's royal purposes as a staging post on

View from where the inner barbican stood in medieval times, looking towards the main gate of the Castle, c.1280. Runnels for the portcullis and a recess for the drawbridge and its chain slits still exist. Machicolations (wall built out on corbels with holes between them through which missiles could be dropped) at roof level were added in the 1380s.

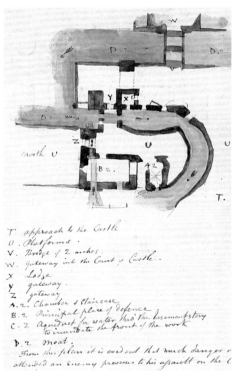

T. approach to the Castle
U. Platforms.
V. Bridge of 2 arches.
W. gateway into the Court of Castle.
X. Lodge
Y. gateway.
Z. gateway
A.2. Chamber & Staircase
B.2. Principal place of defence
C.2. Aqueduct for water thro' the basement story
    to inundate the front of the work
D.2. moat.
From this plan it is evident that much danger &
attended an enemy previous to his assault on the C

In 1798 Thomas Charles
(1777–1855) painted a
watercolour of the mill ruins
and an accurate plan of the
intricate defensive waterworks
of the barbican.

journeys to and from the Continent. Leeds was well placed, being a day's horse ride from London and the coast.

Queen Eleanor died in 1290, moving the king to write, 'My harp is turned to mourning, in life I loved her dearly, nor can I cease to love her in death'. In her memory, he established a chantry at the castle where four canons and a clerk, supplied by Leeds Priory founded by Robert de Crèvecoeur, celebrated mass daily for the repose of her soul. The Chantry was confirmed and extended by Edward III, Richard II, Henry VI and Henry VII.

In 1299, in order to improve relations with France, Edward married Margaret, the sister of Philip the III *le Hardi*, King of France, and they spent their honeymoon at Leeds Castle. The king granted Leeds to his queen, inaugurating the custom whereby the castle became part of the dower of the queens and was retained by them during their widowhood. So from the earliest days of royal ownership ladies played a great part in the history of Leeds.

Edward II, without informing his queen Isabella, the daughter of Philip IV *le Bel*, King of France, granted the castle to Bartholomew, 1st Lord Badlesmere, Lord Steward of the Household, an able and ambitious nobleman who later joined the conspiracies of the northern barons. When Queen Isabella sought shelter for the night at Leeds Castle in the autumn of 1321, she was refused admission by the castellan who ordered his archers to fire on the royal party, killing several of her guards. The king's response was to raise a feudal levy of local men and besiege the castle, which was captured on 1 November. Lord Badlesmere was taken the following year and beheaded. Following the deposition and murder of Edward II in 1327, Queen Isabella caused Parliament to grant her Leeds Castle again, retaining it until her death in 1358. Queen Isabella, accompanied by her daughter Joan of Scotland, wife of David II of Scotland (1324–71), arrived at Leeds Castle on 13 June 1358, following a pilgrimage to Canterbury, and remained until 2 July. When the royal party left the castle Queen Isabella's course was almost run. She died at Hertford on 22 August.

After the queen's death, Edward III carried out continuous works and enlarged the park. This work was supervised by William of Wykeham, founder of New College, Oxford and Winchester College. The chambers of the king and queen in the Gloriette were leaded and plastered. Towards the end of the fourteenth century the works at Leeds Castle were supervised by Henry Yevele, the famous architect who was responsible for the nave of Canterbury Cathedral and the roof of Westminster Hall.

The Fountain Court, the central courtyard of the Gloriette, dates from the 1280s. In the fourteenth century a system was devised for bringing piped water from springs in the park into cisterns beneath the paving to supply the fountain. The same springs supply the Castle today.

Richard II also loved Leeds Castle and granted it to his queen, Anne of Bohemia, in 1382. On her arrival at Dover in December 1381, Queen Anne had been met by John of Gaunt, Duke of Lancaster, and conducted to Leeds where she remained for the Christmas season. Even after the queen's untimely death in 1394, Richard was often there with the Court and Privy Council, transacting state business. Here too, in 1395, he received the famous historian Sir John Froissart, a first edition of whose *Chronicles* is at the castle. After the death of his patron, the Queen of France, Froissart came to Dover and then to Canterbury where he wrote: 'I heard that the King had gone into a beautiful Palace in Kent called Leeds Castle', and went on to describe his reception there.

After his deposition, Richard was brought to Leeds disguised as a forester and lodged there a short time before being removed to Pontefract. Leeds therefore saw Richard II both in his days of power and in his humiliation.

Tumultuous times – the age of Lancaster and York

Henry IV followed tradition by granting Leeds Castle to his second queen, Joan of Navarre, in 1403. During this time the castle underwent a general repair, and the corbels supporting the drawbridge to 'the great tower called the Gloriett' were renewed.

In 1412 Queen Joan granted the castle, with the king's consent, to Thomas Arundel, Archbishop of Canterbury. It was to Leeds that the archbishop summoned Sir John Oldcastle, Lord Cobham, the Lollard leader, to stand trial for heresy. Lord Cobham was excommunicated and later beheaded. In 1414, when Archbishop Arundel died, an inventory was taken and from it we learn for the first time the names of the rooms in the Gloriette.

In 1416 Sigismund, the Holy Roman Emperor, the most powerful sovereign in Europe and also the brother of Anne of Bohemia, came to England on a state visit to Henry V, whose prestige was high after the Battle of Agincourt. Henry made him a Knight of the Garter at Windsor Castle and then on 26 June the king sent his distinguished guest to Leeds Castle where he remained for a month.

Henry V for a time treated his stepmother, Queen Joan, with great consideration. But the wealthy queen, who was avaricious, and her Breton sons from her first marriage to the Duke of Brittany, may have intrigued against Henry V. She had further added to her unpopularity by surrounding herself with foreign courtiers. Suddenly

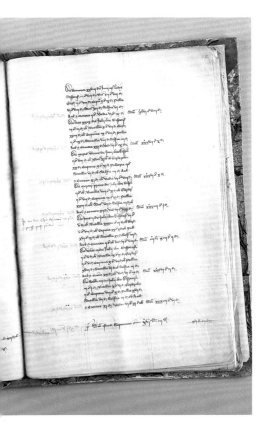

Queen Joan's Wardrobe Book: an account of the day-to-day activities of the widow of Henry IV during her house arrest at Leeds Castle from 8 March to 21 July 1422, with detailed analysis of her personal and household expenses, which included extensive repairs to the castle mill.

she was charged with plotting the king's death by witchcraft by the 'most high and horrible means'. We shall never know precisely what these were because her confessor, who had informed against her, was strangled during a furious altercation with a priest loyal to the queen, enraged by the treachery against her. There was no trial, perhaps because of the death of her accuser, but she was nevertheless imprisoned at Leeds and Pevensey castles. A generation later, in Henry VI's reign the king's aunt, Eleanor Cobham, Duchess of Gloucester, wife of the Lord Protector of the Realm, was also accused of plotting against the life of the king by witchcraft and imprisoned at Leeds Castle. This time the charge was upheld at a trial in St Stephen's Chapel, Westminster. Later, after being remanded from Leeds Castle, Eleanor Cobham was formally condemned as a witch by Henry Chichele, Archbishop of Canterbury.

There is strong presumptive evidence that in both these cases the charges of witchcraft were trumped up for political reasons. In 1419 Henry V had been acutely short of money for his French wars and coveted the wealth of Queen Joan. The seizure of her income of 10,000 marks added as much as ten per cent to the general revenues of the kingdom. Shortly before his death the king repented and ordered her immediate release and full restoration of all her property and dignities, after which she lived peacefully and prosperously for many years. Queen Joan's detailed housekeeping accounts at Leeds Castle for 136 days in the year 1422 are now on display at the castle.

The last queen to hold Leeds Castle personally was Catherine de Valois, widow of Henry V. She was the younger sister of Isabella of France, Richard II's second queen. Receiving the castle in 1422, she immediately gave orders for the repair of the hall and other buildings. There is an inventory of this time which gives details of the prince's chamber in the Gloriette, the study, the cloisters and the steward's chamber.

It was during Queen Catherine's time that the castle's bell and clock dating from 1435 were installed. One of the oldest in the country, it strikes the hours and was rung specially when Her Majesty Queen Elizabeth II visited Leeds Castle in March 1981.

When Henry V died the queen was a lively young girl of twenty-one and she soon fell in love with Owen Tudor, a Welsh courtier who as Clerk of her Wardrobe looked after her dresses and jewels. The gardens and park of Leeds Castle may possibly have become the setting for a royal romance. But when the couple's relationship was discovered, they were both imprisoned. The Queen Dowager, however, was later released and Owen Tudor escaped from Newgate

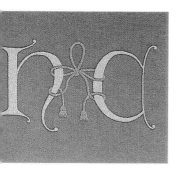

The silk wall and bed hangings in the Queen's Room at Leeds Castle are worked with the initials HC for Henry V and his queen, Catherine de Valois, linked by a lover's knot.

prison. They had, in fact been secretly married and it was their son Edmund, Earl of Richmond, who was later to be the father of Henry VII. Thus they provided England with the remarkable Tudor dynasty whose power was established by Henry Tudor at the Battle of Bosworth Field in 1485.

Henry VIII at Leeds Castle

Henry VIII, most famous of all the owners of Leeds Castle, expended large sums in enlarging and beautifying the whole range of buildings. At the same time he carefully retained the defences of the castle, for he often had cause to fear invasion from either France or the Spanish Netherlands. The king entrusted the work of alteration to his great friend Sir Henry Guildford. They both delighted in jousts and masques and shared intellectual tastes with Erasmus, the great Renaissance Humanist. Sir Henry, appointed Constable and Parker of Leeds in 1512, was also a Knight of the Garter, Master of the Horse and Comptroller of the Royal Household and a Member of Parliament. Improvements made by Sir Henry for the king were by far the most important since those carried out by Edward III, who had rendered Leeds Castle into 'a beautiful palace'. He transformed the Gloriette, superimposing canted bay windows of sixteen lights in the royal apartments, and thoroughly repaired the royal rooms.

The Maiden's Tower, reconstructed in Tudor times to house, it is said, royal maids-of-honour. The nineteenth-century name refers to the recluse Christina Hyde, who lived here in the reign of Richard II. The crenellations were added in the late 18th century.

With an entourage of 3,997 people, the king set out from Greenwich on his way to the meeting at the Field of the Cloth of Gold, on Sunday 21 May 1520, reaching Leeds Castle the next day. Queen Catherine travelled in the same glittering cavalcade accompanied by a personal suite of 1,175 people. Not all of this vast concourse would have been lodged within the castle but most certainly the Cardinal of York, Thomas Wolsey, and nine other bishops would have. The queen would have enjoyed her new apartments. Final arrangements for the surprise visit to this country of the Holy Roman Emperor Charles V were doubtless discussed by the king and Wolsey, who had charge of all the arrangements both for the meeting with the emperor and with the French king at the Field of the Cloth of Gold.

Leeds Castle has ever been a haven. To avoid an outbreak of the sweating sickness during the summer of 1528, Cardinal Wolsey retired to the castle where he spent much time sifting the rush for dead men's lands and offices precipitated by the epidemic. He would also, at this time, have devoted much thought on ways to progress the 'king's great matter' – putting away Queen Catherine of Aragon.

In 1544, after the ignominious collapse of the invasion of France by

Henry VIII and Charles V, the Holy Roman Emperor, Henry retreated to England, and with the Privy Council, went straight to Leeds Castle. There the Imperial ambassadors took their leave and, to the general consternation, were not replaced.

Besides his troubles with France and the Empire, Henry VIII had serious problems in Ireland. He appointed to govern Ireland as Lord Deputy 'a wise and warie gentleman', Sir Anthony St Leger. He

Henry VIII, whose portrait by an unknown English artist hangs in the Henry VIII Banqueting Hall in the Castle, undertook wholesale restoration and enlargement in the years 1517–23.

pursued a conciliatory policy with the Irish, who, as a result, agreed for the first time to accept the occupant of the English throne as King of Ireland. Sir Anthony's services were much valued by both Henry VIII and his successor Edward VI. In recognition of this, in 1552, the Lord Protector and the Council granted Leeds Castle to Sir Anthony, who was Lord of the Manor of Ulcombe nearby.

Leeds Castle thus passed out of royal ownership. For some three hundred years it had been an occasional residence for the medieval kings and queens of England, many of whom loved it greatly. Three of the queens who held it were French princesses who brought with them the refined luxury for which the beautiful castles of the French royal family were famous. But Leeds Castle, especially after the improvements made by Henry VIII, could rival the beauty of these legendary French castles, most of which exist no more.

From Jacobean to 'Gothick'

Sir Anthony St Leger's son, Sir Warham, High Sheriff of Kent in 1560, was appointed Governor of Munster in 1565. In 1570 he imprisoned at Leeds the Earl of Desmond and his family who had rebelled against the Crown in Munster. His son Anthony St Leger lived at Leeds, but his grandson, also Sir Warham, was not so fortunate. A financial backer of Sir Walter Raleigh's ill-fated expedition to discover the legendary gold of El Dorado, he was ruined when the venture ended in disaster and was forced to sell the castle to his wife's uncle, Sir Richard Smythe, in 1618.

Although the Smythe family were not long at the castle they did rebuild the principal buildings at the north end of the main island. Their fine Jacobean house, the footings of which were discovered within the present building during repair work in 1993, survived unaltered until the middle of the eighteenth century. Of the rooms the grandest was the saloon which had a finely carved ceiling. Passing through the female line, the castle was sold in 1632 to a St Leger connection, Sir Thomas Culpeper of Hollingbourne, who settled it on his eldest son, Sir Cheney, who later took the side of Parliament in the struggle with Charles I. During the civil war the castle was used by Parliament as the arsenal for Kent. Because of this and Sir Cheney's inclinations the castle was not rendered indefensible, as were the castles of Corfe and Rochester. Sir Cheney remained in possession until his death in 1663, but the Restoration of 1660 ruined him and he died not only deeply in debt but also intestate.

This painting by an unknown artist, c.1750, shows the handsome Jacobean house, with square-headed windows and leaden spouts, built by the Smythe family, 1618–30.

His cousin, Thomas, 2nd Lord Culpeper, used the dowry of his wealthy wife, Margaret van Hesse, to purchase Leeds Castle from the creditors of Sir Cheney's estate. His father, John, 1st Lord Culpeper, an astute politician and loyal servant of Charles I, had held the offices of both Chancellor of the Exchequer and Master of the Rolls. He had been instrumental in conveying the young Prince of Wales out of England and into exile in France and in 1649 had been rewarded for his loyalty by the gift of a large tract of land in Virginia. This eventually comprised all the land between the Potomac and Rappahanock rivers, more than five million acres for which the yearly rental was £6.13s.4d.

During the 2nd Lord's ownership, but while he was absent from the castle, Leeds was used as a prison for some 600 captured French and Dutch sailors. Lodged in all parts of the building including the Gloriette, on one notable occasion they set fire to their accommodation. This caused so much damage that part of the eastern wall fell into the moat and remained ruinous until 1822. The diarist John Evelyn, Commissioner for Prisoners, wrote to the Duke of Albemarle that, quite apart from the havoc wreaked by the inmates, the castle was in need of repair and proper drains. In 1676, following the failure of Nathaniel Bacon's rebellion in Virginia, the brother of the queen of a tribe of North American Indians was sent to England as a hostage and lodged at Leeds Castle where he was called William. He died in 1678 and was buried at Broomfield on 26 February.

In 1667 Lord Culpeper returned to Leeds but departed again some thirteen years later when, having bought out his co-proprietors in the American estate, he was appointed Governor of Virginia. His daughter, the heiress Catherine, married Thomas, 5th Lord Fairfax in the spring of 1690 and eventually, on the death of Lady Culpeper in 1710, Leeds Castle passed to the Fairfax family which had held the Virginia Proprietary since 1690.

However, the American estate was by no means secure, and over the next half-century there was continual unrest as the settlers and the colonial government challenged the Fairfax ownership. The 6th Lord Fairfax finally achieved confirmation of the family's sole rights in 1745, and then sailed for Virginia, the only peer ever to emigrate to America, handing over Leeds Castle to his brother Robert.

The portraits on this and the preceding page are of related members of the Culpeper and Fairfax families. At the top of page 18: Margaret, Lady Culpeper (1635–1710), née Van Hesse, by Adrian Hanneman. She married Thomas, second Lord Culpeper (1635–89), centre, whose portrait, also by Hanneman, 1664, reveals a man of determined character. Bottom: Lord Culpeper's son-in-law Thomas Fairfax, fifth Lord Fairfax (1657–1710); portrait attributed to John Riley. Above: the Hon. Catherine Culpeper (c.1670–1719), only child of the second Lord Culpeper and his wife, and wife of fifth Lord Fairfax. The King Charles spaniel, in this portrait attributed to Henry Stone or John Hayle, c.1673, is a symbol of the Culpeper's attachment to the House of Stuart.

Robert Fairfax commissioned Thomas Hogben, a schoolmaster at Smarden, to survey and draw this exquisite estate map. Completed in 1748, it shows the park, pleasure grounds, Castle, and field names including the vineyard. At the foot of the map is an accurate panorama of the Castle seen from the west.

Sundial made by Thomas Hogben in 1750. The time at Belvoir, the Fairfax seat on the Potomac in Virginia, is indicated five hours behind Leeds. At Belvoir there was a sundial giving the time at Leeds.

The Virginia Proprietary

When he arrived in Virginia in November 1747, never again to leave its shores, Lord Fairfax stayed first with his cousin William at Belvoir on the banks of the Potomac, a few miles below present day Alexandria, where he became the friend and patron of the fifteen-year-old George Washington. Later Fairfax removed nearer the frontier in order better to supervise the development of his estates. Assigning himself some 150,000 acres, an area larger by far than that of his estate of Leeds Castle, he named the tract 'The Manor of Leeds', building himself a ranch-style house named Greenway Court, a reminder of the original Culpeper home at Hollingbourne near Leeds. Here Lord Fairfax lived quietly until his death in 1781. From time to time he was visited by relations who made the long voyage across the Atlantic to see him. One of his great pleasures was hunting, so he went frequently to Belvoir to follow hounds with George Washington. Though war was to separate the Fairfax and Washington families, General Washington retained his affection and friendship for the family.

Robert Fairfax

When Robert Fairfax became master of Leeds Castle he put in hand a programme of alterations and 'improvements'. The exterior of the Smythe house was altered by introducing fashionable 'Strawberry Hill Gothick' features to the windows and door surrounds. Fairfax's two wives Martha Collins, heiress of the Child banking family, and Dorothy Best, were both wealthy, which was fortunate because

Hon. Robert Fairfax, later seventh Lord Fairfax (1706–93), sometime a major in the Life Guards and lieutenant colonel of the West Kent Militia, wearing a breastplate under a uniform coat; owned Leeds Castle for forty-six years from 1747; portrait by John Vanderbank before 1740.

Leeds Castle after superficial 'Strawberry Hill Gothick' alterations (criticised by Horace Walpole, the creator of Strawberry Hill) were made by Robert Fairfax from the 1750s, as shown in a watercolour, c.1790.

Robert Fairfax was an extravagant man. He sat as MP for Maidstone and for Kent, and succeeded his brother as 7th Lord Fairfax in 1781. King George III and Queen Charlotte came to Leeds in November 1778 after reviewing the army at Coxheath nearby. For the visit Fairfax expended large sums on refurnishing the drawing rooms for the king's and queen's use. At Fairfax's death in 1793 the property passed to his nephew the Revd Dr Denny Martin, who took the name Fairfax, and in 1800 to the latter's brother General Philip Martin.

Details of two views of Leeds Castle drawn by Fiennes Wykeham Martin's daughter, Eliza, later Mrs Simeon. The first (1821) shows the Castle on the eve of its restoration, and the second (1823) its transformation.

In 1806 General Martin sold the Manor of Leeds in Virginia, which had not been confiscated at the Revolution, for £14,000. He also received £20,000 in compensation for the loss of the Proprietary itself; and on his death in August 1821 his fortune was left to his distant kinsman Fiennes Wykeham, of Chacombe Priory, Northamptonshire, who added Martin to his surname. It so happened that Wykeham Martin was descended from William, 1st Lord Leyburn, who conveyed the castle to Edward I and Eleanor of Castile.

Fiennes Wykeham Martin and the restoration of the medieval style

Wykeham Martin's architect, William Baskett, of Camberwell, who had worked on several houses in Norfolk, demolished Sir Richard Smythe's Jacobean house and built one in the style of Henry VII, closely resembling the great gatehouse of Titchfield Abbey on Southampton Water. The foundation stones of the turrets of the main tower were laid on 15 May 1822. Less than four months later the roof was raised on 11 September, Charles Wykeham Martin's twenty-first birthday. The following year Baskett began work on restoring the medieval Gloriette and Tudor Maiden's Tower, and by 1824 the castle had taken on more or less the external appearance it has today. Lord Conway, the architectural historian, in judging the effect of this restoration concluded; 'It possesses one great merit . . . it enters perfectly into the general complex of the whole.'

With the completion of Mr Baskett's works, Fiennes Wykeham Martin had expended some £33,955 on the project and on the park improvements carried out between 1823 and 1825 – a sum approaching £3 million in today's terms. The current layout of the park, with the exception of the Duckery, the Wood Garden, the Pavilion Garden and the Culpeper Garden, dates from the Wykeham Martin era. The moat, in a sorry state for many years, also took on its present appearance. New drives were cut and the principal entrance was altered to strike the Maidstone–Folkestone road where it does today.

One of the first important visitors to see the newly erected castle was the Duchess of Kent, Queen Victoria's mother. In an undated letter at the end of the 1820s, Charles Wykeham Martin wrote in haste to his father: 'The Duchess of Kent will pass through the Park tomorrow on her way to Lord Liverpool's (at Buxted Park), the gates should be open. It will not be necessary for anyone to show themselves & perhaps better not to stop the carriage as she will be in a hurry.'

Many possessions of previous owners left Leeds around this period. During the 1820s Fiennes Wykeham Martin faced financial difficulties due to the cost of his work at Leeds. It became necessary to sell the contents of the castle to meet his most pressing creditors. In 1830 Christie's organised a sale of furniture and pictures which are now widely dispersed. In January of the following year the splendid library was also sold. Wykeham Martin also gave to the Smythes, by now Viscounts Strangford, all their family portraits. These appear to have been lost.

Two of a charming series of watercolour views of Leeds Castle by the antiquarian Edward Pretty:
The first shows the Castle from the east; the damage caused by the Dutch prisoners in the 1660s, and the vane now on the pavilion in the Duckery, can be seen.

After the rebuilding and restoration of the fabric, the Wykeham Martins settled to a century of ownership. When the Leeds Abbey estate was sold in 1839 the trustees of General Martin's will secured it and added it to the Leeds Castle estate. Charles Wykeham Martin restored the family fortunes by his first marriage to the heiress Lady Jemima Mann, daughter of the last Earl Cornwallis, which linked him to all the leading families in Kent. He was a Member of Parliament, and in his old age wrote a history of the castle. His second wife, Matilda, was a cousin of the novelist Anthony Trollope, who became an occasional visitor to the castle, and it is tempting to picture Leeds as the inspiration for Courcy Castle in the Barsetshire novels. Charles's son, Philip, also a Member of Parliament, died in 1878, and his trustees purchased the lower part of the Duppa Estate at Hollingbourne when it was sold in 1895. The acquisition of two valuable estates during the nineteenth century made the Leeds Castle estate the largest in central Kent.

Second watercolour by Edward Pretty showing the ruins of the mill looking towards the machicolation above the main gate.

Visitors were always welcome at the castle in groups, long before its official opening in 1976. In 1874 a small dining club of the Royal Institute of British Architects came to Leeds. Among the members of that summer excursion were F.P. Cockerell, J.H. Christian, Digby Wyatt, George Aitchison, J.L. Pearson, William Burges and Alfred Waterhouse. There is unfortunately no record of what this august group of architects thought of Mr Baskett's work at Leeds. In August 1882 the castle witnessed the spectacle of upwards of 400 members of the Kent Archaeological Society arriving at the castle by carriage.

Modern times; the achievement of Lady Baillie

With the death of Cornwallis Wykeham Martin in 1924 the family was faced with such heavy death duties that the decision was made to sell and the property was put on the market. Among the prospective buyers was Randolph Hearst, the American newspaper tycoon. 'WANT BUY CASTLE IN ENGLAND', read his telegram to his English agent, 'PLEASE FIND WHICH ONES AVAILABLE.' Unfortunately the report which went back to him after Leeds had been inspected was not favourable: 'QUITE UNIQUE AS ANTIQUITY BUT NEEDS EXPENDITURE LARGE SUM TO MAKE IT HABITABLE NOT A BATH IN PLACE ONLY LIGHTING OIL LAMPS SERVANTS QUARTERS DOWN DUNGEONS . . .' Hearst looked elsewhere, and in 1926 Leeds was bought by the Hon. Mrs Wilson-Filmer, who saw through any disadvantages to the castle's true charm and character.

Detail of the entablature in the Yellow Drawing Room enhanced by lambrequins designed by Stéphane Boudin, which are continued across the windows as valances.

Lady Baillie, as she became, immediately set about the restoration of the castle with characteristic imagination and vigour, completely renovating the basic structure and restoring the Gloriette, where the most important apartments of the medieval kings and queens had been. Anglo-American by birth, Lady Baillie was the eldest daughter of Almeric Paget, Lord Queenborough, GBE, and his wife, Pauline, daughter and heiress of the Hon. William Whitney, United States Navy Secretary in President Cleveland's first administration. Her father was the grandson of Field Marshal the Marquess of Anglesey, KG, cavalry commander at Waterloo, whose ancestor, William, 1st Lord Paget, KG, was one of Henry VIII's executors and principal Secretaries of State. Lady Baillie had spent part of her early life in France, and to that country she turned instinctively for the designers who would transform Leeds for her. The first of these, Armand-Albert Rateau, made a French Gothic fantasy of the Gloriette but it was Stéphane Boudin who, in the 1930s, began the task of restoring the internal harmony of the main building. Boundless enjoyment went into the decorating and furnishing of Leeds over almost thirty years, as shopping expeditions to Paris and London, endless supplies of samples and catalogues, and long discussions finally produced the classic elegance of these rooms as we see them today. Lady Baillie created the Wood Garden, bordered by the little streams of the River Len, and brought rare birds from all over the world for the gardens and lakes. Apart from the love of her children and the welfare of her staff, the embellishment of Leeds Castle became her life's work. She lived at Leeds Castle longer than any other owner in all its recorded history, and her work for the castle ranks with that of Edward I and Eleanor of Castile, Edward III, Henry VIII and Fiennes Wykeham Martin.

Under her care Leeds Castle became, in the 1930s, one of the great houses of England and a centre of lavish hospitality. Visitors included Queen Marie of Roumania, grand-daughter of Queen Victoria, born at Eastwell Park near Ashford, Alfonso XIII of Spain, and from the British royal family the Prince of Wales, afterwards Edward VIII and Duke of Windsor, the Duke of Kent and his wife Princess Marina of Greece. Other guests were ambassadors, ministers, Members of Parliament, and art collectors such as Sir Alfred Beit. Lady Baillie greatly enjoyed motion pictures so it is natural for her to have entertained such stars of the screen as Douglas Fairbanks, Errol Flynn, James Stewart and Douglas Fairbanks Jr – all people from different backgrounds but who in their several ways made their hostess's residence a house of distinction. But Lady Baillie was very shy and particularly disliked any personal publicity; and so Leeds Castle, in spite of its importance, was very seldom in the news.

During the second world war, Leeds figured importantly, albeit secretly, in the defence of England at her most vulnerable point, the Channel ports, which were under constant threat of invasion. The secret Petroleum Warfare Department was established to develop flame-throwing weapons, and it was from Leeds that operations were directed, largely through Geoffrey Lloyd (later Lord Geoffrey-Lloyd) reporting direct to Winston Churchill. Because the Len valley is a natural fog-trap at Leeds, Geoffrey-Lloyd used it for the experiments which perfected 'FIDO' (Fog Investigation Dispersal Operations), which resulted in the saving of many airmen's lives when landing in fog. It was his most satisfying wartime achievement.

Coat of arms of Lady Baillie's family, the Pagets.

For some years Lady Baillie lent the castle as a military hospital and herself organised a convalescent home for badly burned pilots who had been treated by the famous plastic surgeon, Sir Archibald McIndoe, at East Grinstead Hospital.

After the war, Lady Baillie lived a quiet family life and devoted herself more and more to the preservation of the castle for posterity. During her last illness she worked with utter determination to achieve her final purpose: to give Leeds Castle to the nation in perpetuity.

To mark the part played by ladies as owners of the Castle, the flag of Eleanor of Castile, the first queen to hold Leeds Castle, flies from the masthead on the tower of the Gloriette in alternation with the flag of the last personal owner of Leeds Castle, the Hon. Olive, Lady Baillie, who gave the Castle for the British people's enjoyment for ever.

Etienne Drian's portrait of Lady Baillie and her daughters, Susan (left) and the late Pauline (right), seated in the western bay window of the Thorpe Hall Room; painted in 1947.

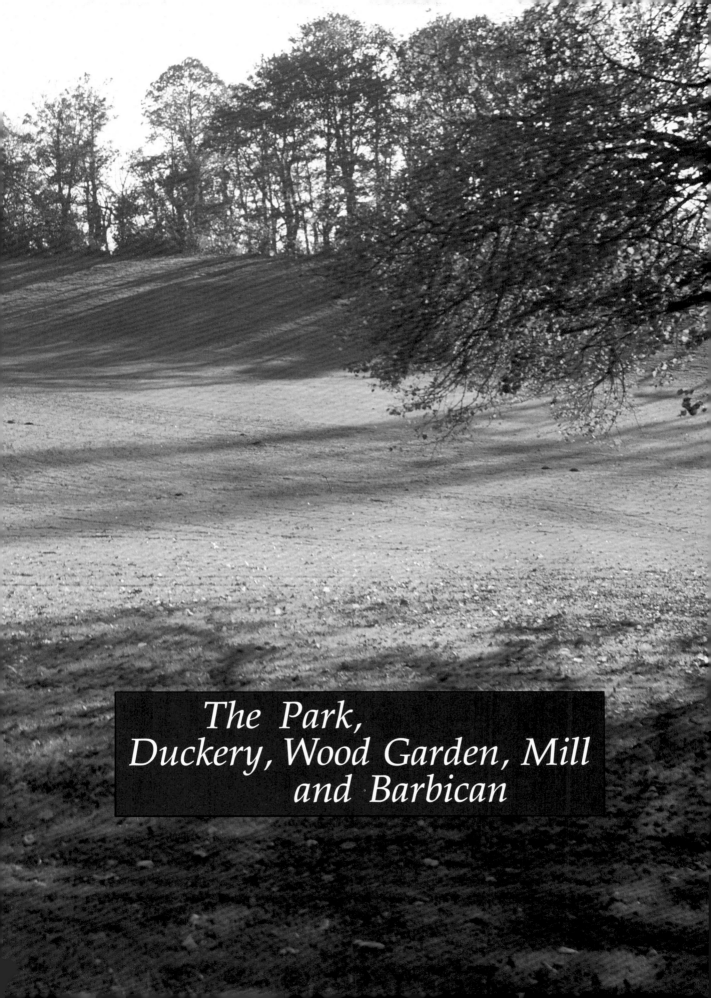

The Park,
Duckery, Wood Garden, Mill
and Barbican

Leeds Castle provides a panorama of architecture from the twelfth to the twentieth centuries. On the extreme left of the picture is the thirteenth-century keep or Gloriette, its walls rising sheer from the water, and connected to the main island by stone bridge corridors. The main island is bounded on the west side (shown nearest) by a revetment wall with two drum bastions, dating from c.1280. At the north end of the island is the main part of the Castle, rebuilt in the nineteenth century to replace a Jacobean building, which in turn had replaced medieval buildings. The Maiden's Tower, the square building on the east side, is late Tudor, while the group of buildings at the south end through which the entrance road passes dates from the thirteenth century. The Gatehouse is a late Norman structure improved upon by Edward I (see page 61).

THE PARK

At the close of the seventeenth century Leeds Castle was owned by Margaret, Lady Culpeper, who with her son-in-law, Thomas, 5th Lord Fairfax, gave to the park the formal appearance recorded on the estate map of 1748 (see pages 20–21). Some oaks, estimated to have been planted between 1710 and 1740, survive from this period. Plantings took place at intervals throughout the eighteenth century and more particularly after the heavy storms of the winter of 1826–27. Since the great storm of October 1987, many new trees have been planted to restore the eighteenth-century plan and to create some new avenues.

THE DUCKERY, WOOD GARDEN, MILL AND BARBICAN

From the car park visitors come first to the Duckery, which was created in the 1960s for Lady Baillie by Stéphane Boudin and the international garden designer, Russell Page, out of a wilderness of tangled brambles and fallen trees. Further work in 1990 tidied the banks and added resting places. It is a perfect habitat for the fine collection of waterfowl, ranging from mallard and teal to rare geese and black swans, which roam freely throughout the grounds of the Castle, including the golf course. The shaded seat in the small pavilion affords one of the most beautiful views of the Castle.

At the head of the cascade, built in 1827, the path leads past two ponds known to have been here since at least 1086 when there was a mill, to the Wood Garden; cedar trees date from about 1840–50. The first landscaping of this area was done in the 1920s, to make the most of the natural beauty of the streams of the River Len. It was conceived from the start as a 'green garden', and more particularly as a 'Spring Garden', when great masses of daffodils, narcissi and anemones planted among the ash, willows and alder burst into colour. At the end of the paths, the Castle comes into view, set like a jewel in the lake which has surrounded it since the mid-thirteenth century. Next to the Pavilion Garden water levels have been changed and the landscape much altered. A mill and its pond were located here in the fourteenth century, but by the eighteenth the mill pond had become a canal draining away over a cascade to the meandering streams. Rhododendrons have been grown in this part of the park since the 1870s.

In recent years, following the general design of François Goffinet, both sides of the River Len have been improved and replanted and the woodland garden redeveloped and made more colourful. Hydrangea, rhododendron and azalea beds have been added to the Pavilion Garden.

The Castle can be approached from three directions, all originally leading through the barbican (see page 8). Dating from the late thirteenth century the barbican and fortified flour mill are without parallel in Great Britain. During excavations between 1985 and 1989 the mill wheel and cogwheel pits were restored to their original proportions.

Ringed Teal
(Anas leucophrys)

Shelduck
(Tadorna tadorna)

Ne-ne or Hawaiian Geese (Branta sandvicensis)

The Castle Within

To Terrace Room and Fairfax Hall Restaurant, Toilets,
Castle Shop & Country Clothing Shop, Culpeper Garden, Av
Maze & Grotto, Greenhouses, Plant Shop & Vineyard

GREAT WATER

Guardroom

Gate Tower

Maiden's Tower

Inner Bailey

Low Level

17

Curtain Wall

16

Sundial

15

Main Castle

Toilets

2

12

14

Outer Bailey

13

11

1

MOAT
Fed by the River Len

3

4

6

9

7

8

10

Gloriette

5

N

Fortified Mill

PLAN OF LEEDS CASTLE

1 ENTRANCE TO CELLAR
2 HERALDRY ROOM
3 QUEEN'S ROOM
4 QUEEN'S BATHROOM
5 QUEEN'S GALLERY
6 HENRY VIII BANQUETING HALL
7 CHAPEL
8 FOUNTAIN COURT
9 GOTHIC STAIRCASE
10 SEMINAR ROOM
11 UPPER CORRIDOR
12 MAIN STAIRCASE
13 YELLOW DRAWING ROOM
14 THORPE HALL ROOM
15 INNER HALL
16 ENTRANCE HALL
17 DOG COLLAR MUSEUM

THE CELLAR

The cellar, beneath the late Georgian house of 1822, is the oldest surviving visible part of the Castle, and shows Norman influence, dating from the mid-twelfth century or later. It runs the whole depth of the building, and traces of an entrance from the bailey can be seen. A blocked stone staircase, formerly leading to the Great Hall above, can be seen in the right wall. Being dry and cool, it is an eminently suitable place for the storage of wine, for which it was probably used from earliest times. Wine used for conferences in the castle, including the estate's own wine, can be seen stored in the cellar.

THE HERALDRY ROOM

This room was originally the site of the great hall of the medieval castle. The 1822 rebuilding retained the great hall right up to the front hall. In 1927, Lady Baillie's architect, Owen Little, turned the room into a library. He installed the present handsome plaster ceiling made from moulds from Jacobean originals, supplied by the well known building firm White Allom.

The Heraldry Room takes its name from the coats of arms of the owners of Leeds, which are displayed on the walls together with portraits of royal owners. The arms of some of the principal owners are shown here. Heraldry has been termed 'the shorthand of history', although the use of individual badges and emblems on the armour and accoutrements of sovereigns and their noble and knightly subjects did not emerge until the mid-twelfth century. By the third crusade (1189), there was a system to distinguish one family or person from another heraldically, and heralds, experts in the idiosyncrasies of the system, came into being. The heralds marshalled tournaments and organised the ceremonial aspects of marriages and funerals, all occasions coloured by heraldry. The system of quartering, whereby two or more shields are 'marshalled' together in one shield, indicates that the bearer represents two or more families. Examples in the room include the lions of England quartering the fleurs-de-lys of France, and the Wykeham chevronels and roses quartering the Martin lions rampant.

In the other showcases are displayed various documents of historical importance to Leeds Castle.

Crèvecoeur 1090–1268
Or (gold background colour of shield first) a cross voided gules (red – colour of charges second). This shield appears to have been used also by Leeds Abbey, founded in 1119 by Robert de Crèvecoeur one mile south of the castle.

St Leger 1552–1618
Azure fretty argent (silver, diagonal crossing lines) a chief (top third of shield) or. These arms are currently borne by the St Leger family whose head is Viscount Doneraile.

Royal Family 1290–1340

Gules three lions passant (walking) guardant (head turned to the left) in pale (one above another) or. These became the established arms of England.

Royal Family 1340–1407

Quarterly 1 and 4, Azure (blue) semé-de-lys (all over fleurs-de-lys) or (for France); 2 and 3, Three lions passant guardant or (for England). Edward III quartered the French royal arms from 1340 as the nearest male heir to his uncle King Charles IV of France.

Royal Family 1407–1522

Quarterly 1 and 4, Azure three fleurs-de-lys or for France; 2 and 3, England. The three fleurs-de-lys were adopted in 1407 by Henry IV for a new Great Seal and these French arms were borne by English sovereigns until the Union with Ireland in 1801, when George III abandoned title of King of France.

Culpeper 1632–1710

Argent a bend engrailed gules. These arms were borne since at least the thirteenth century by a family ubiquitous throughout Kent and Sussex.

Fairfax 1710–1793

Or three bars gemels (pairs of small parallel lines) gules surmounted by a lion rampant sable (black). These arms are currently borne by Lord Fairfax of Cameron and his family.

Wykeham Martin 1821–1926

Quarterly 1 and 4, Gules a lion rampant encircled by crosses crosslet and mullets (5 pointed spur rowels) alternately or (for Martin); 2 and 3, Argent two chevronels between three roses gules (for Wykeham). When he inherited Leeds Castle from General Martin, Fiennes Wykeham adopted the additional name and arms of Martin by Royal Licence in 1821, as representative of both families.

THE QUEEN'S ROOM

This room and the Queen's Bathroom are prepared as they might have been for Henry V's queen, Catherine de Valois, in the year 1430.

The medieval state bed was distinguished from other beds by its hangings rather than construction. Before the queen arrived, the royal hangings – a richly embroidered tester and curtains of the same material – were suspended from the ceiling over the bed-frame already there. A medieval great chamber was also a private dining, reception and audience room. Beds were used as seats, with curtains looped up as illustrated below; the conical 'sparver' canopy, denoting rank, of the day-bed is shown on the left. Symbolism was important in furniture and decoration: the raised state chair and golden crown surmounting the canopy of the day-bed ensured a prominent position for the queen. On the bed hangings and the damask covering the walls the monogram HC entwined with a lover's knot represents the union and desired peace between England and France through the marriage of Henry V and Catherine de Valois. The chimneypiece was originally in the Henry VIII Banqueting Hall and its spandrels contain Tudor heraldry.

Authentic reconstruction based on illustration of room of Isabel of Bavaria, Queen of France, mother of Catherine de Valois, Henry V's queen. From a Burgundian manuscript in the British Library (Harley MS 4431).

THE QUEEN'S BATHROOM

Small and comfortable, with a fireplace, the Queen's Bathroom shows the kind of arrangements made for bathing in any place where a stone bath was not a permanent fixture. Etiquette and courtly splendour were just as important in the bathroom as anywhere else, and here again the walls are hung with damask. The design matches that of the fabric in the main room but here it is worked in green and red. Like the state bed, the bath itself is surprisingly humble beneath its hangings – a simple wooden cooper's tub, standing on a rush mat. The tub is surrounded by a fine white circular curtain which hangs from a sparver canopy, again denoting rank, suspended from the ceiling. Like the state bed, this was all designed to be easily dismantled when the queen was not in residence. The towels hanging over the sides of the bath are of the finest white linen and were intended to protect the royal user from the rough wood surface. Inside the bath is a wooden stool, also draped in linen, for the queen to sit on, and another stands outside to assist her in stepping in and out. The bath would have been filled with herb-scented water, carried up from the kitchens in wooden buckets, and emptied through the tap which can be seen at the base.

THE QUEEN'S GALLERY

The Queen's Gallery, leading into the Fountain Court (see page 11), is mentioned as early as 1414 when it was furnished with two cupboards, one screen and two benches. Now it houses examples of oak furniture from the Tudor and later periods. In earlier centuries it was used as an assembly room and, with the adjoining cloister which once surrounded the Fountain Court, as a place for promenading during poor weather. It was also used for the Court of the Hundred of Eyhorne, the feudal administrative area in which the manor of Leeds is situated, and from 1822 to 1924 it formed part of the domestic offices. Lady Baillie brought it back into use as a reception room.

The Queen's Gallery has an interesting fireplace, formerly in the Queen's Withdrawing Room above the Banqueting Hall, with heraldic devices in the spandrels. On the right are a castle, emblem of Castile and pomegranates, emblem of Aragon. These indicate that the fireplace was built before Catherine of Aragon fell into disfavour. Catherine's father Ferdinand V, *The Catholic*, King of Aragon, was also King of Castile and Leon in right of his wife, hence his daughter's use of both badges. The Castile castle is seen elsewhere in the arms of Edward I's first wife, Eleanor of Castile. On the left are the royal arms of the House of Lancaster from whom the Tudor dynasty descended. The winged dragon, associated with the Tudors, is also clearly defined.

Windows in the Gallery date from the thirteenth century, and they look out over the park and moat. The heavy oak beams of the ceiling were introduced by Lady Baillie, and carved by modern French craftsmen working under the direction of Armand-Albert Rateau.

HENRY VIII BANQUETING HALL

The Henry VIII Banqueting Hall, with its superb ebony wood floor and carved oak ceiling, both introduced by Lady Baillie, runs a length of seventy-two feet between the Gallery and the Chapel. The bay window dates from Sir Henry Guildford's supervision of rebuilding for Henry VIII in 1517. The long oak table, partly seventeenth-century and possibly from an Italian monastery, has eight drawers and six legs arranged in an H. The interesting sixteenth-century chimneypiece is French, carved with medallion busts in relief, and was installed by Lady Baillie during the extensive rebuilding of 1927–28, while the armorial iron fireback is one of the earliest in England, dating perhaps from Edward IV. On the chimneypiece stand a seventeenth-century East Mediterranean vase and tankard with mother-of-pearl inlay. In front of it is a group of fifteenth-century Italian *Savonarola* armchairs. To the left of the fireplace is a very rare early Enghien armorial tapestry of 1528–35, with the arms of Antoine de Jauche, Bailli d'Enghien. To the right is a mid-sixteenth-century Flemish verdure tapestry. In one of the two portraits of Richard II, the 1st Lord Lumley is petitioning the king for permission to crenellate his castle in 1392.

THE CHAPEL

The Chapel, rededicated in 1978 by the Archbishop of Canterbury, is a simple room dating from the thirteenth century. The walls are hung with Venetian canvas printed locally with a Gothic design. Behind the altar is a fine late fifteenth-century Flemish tapestry depicting the Adoration of the Magi. Four wooden panels, depicting the Annunciation, the Birth of Christ, the Adoration and the Circumcision, are probably the early sixteenth-century work of Ulm carvers. The silver cross on the altar was donated by the Royal College of Nursing. The late eighteenth-century organ, cased in mahogany, with lime carvings, was purchased by the Leeds Castle Foundation in 1980.

THE STAIRCASE

The sixteenth-century staircase was brought from France by Lady Baillie to give access to the first floor. It is built entirely of oak, with a spirally ribbed newel post formed from a single tree trunk, up which crawls a carved salamander. The post is surmounted by a laughing crusader and his dog. A group of sketches by Constantin Guys, whose vignettes of fashionable society in nineteenth-century Paris reflect the flamboyance and extravagance of the Second Empire, hangs in the landing at the head of the stairs. The corridor that follows contains paintings of Lady Baillie's birds by Philip Rickman (1891–1982), and passes private rooms, including the Board Room used for conferences.

THE SEMINAR ROOM

After French and Dutch prisoners damaged the Gloriette by fire in the 1660s, this room remained ruined until its restoration in 1822, from which date until 1924 it was used as a billiard room. In 1927 it was arranged as Lady Baillie's boudoir; photographs of the time show the extremely ornate gilded panelling which was introduced. Since the establishment of the Leeds Castle Foundation, the room was for a time used for important seminars and conferences, having been redecorated to display

the residue of Lady Baillie's impressionist collection, including paintings by Segonzac and Brianchon, two twentieth-century artists she favoured in her later years as a collector.

The room contains the only portrait ever painted of Lady Baillie (Etienne Drian, 1947), with her two daughters, Susan (left) and the late Pauline (right). They are depicted in the bay window of the Thorpe Hall Room (see page 56). In the windows are bronze figures of the nursing pioneer Florence Nightingale and of the Hon. Olive Paget (later Lady Baillie) as a wartime nurse in 1918.

Seated on the chimneypiece is a cat-shaped bronze mummy case, copied from the original of 600BC, loaned to Leeds Castle until 1996. In ancient Egypt cats were sacred to the god Bast, whose cult was centred at Bubastis.

The upper floor of the Gloriette, when first built, was made over entirely to the queen's use. Emblems associated with Catherine of Aragon were features of several of the rooms. As visitors leave the Seminar Room they pass private rooms on their right which were originally Queen Catherine's withdrawing room and bedroom, and, in Lady Baillie's time, her bedroom.

THE CORRIDOR AND MAIN STAIRCASE

The bridge corridor linking the two parts of the Castle dates from 1822, when it replaced a lath and plaster screen erected by the Fairfax family. On the walls hang pictures by William Hayes, a leading British ornithologist and bird artist at the end of the eighteenth century, and portraits by Thomas P. Earl of *Golden Miller* and *Insurance*, two legendary racehorses owned by Lady Baillie's sister, the Hon. Dorothy Paget.

The corridor leads onto a half-landing on the main staircase, reconstructed by Boudin. Rateau replaced a top light above the staircase with a beamed ceiling in the French – Gothic style he introduced in the Gloriette (see page 25). On the first floor wall opposite is a portrait of the Hon. Catherine Culpeper, heiress of Leeds, as a girl (see page 19). In the stairwell below are portraits of Lady Baillie's father, Lord Queenborough, and her American mother Pauline (*née* Whitney).

Below the half-landing Lady Baillie installed the carved marble coat of arms of a Spanish grandee and member of the Aragon family, the Duke of Segorbe and

Cardona, a Knight of the Golden Fleece, who died in 1670. At either side of the central screen arch is a pair of wrought iron Neo-Gothic torchères, sixteenth-century stands supporting pricket candlesticks.

The four tapestries hanging on the main staircase were woven by Michael Wauters at Brussels in the late seventeenth century. They were commissioned by William Cavendish, 1st Duke of Newcastle, KG, *The Loyal Duke*, and Royalist general (*c*.1595–1676), and formerly hung at his seat Welbeck Abbey in Nottinghamshire.

The two tapestries on the upper flight show Captain Mazin, equerry to King Charles II and riding instructor, practising dressage movements, with Bolsover Castle, a property of the Duke of Newcastle, in the background. The tapestry over the half-landing is of the duke himself, bareheaded, in armour, riding a prancing chestnut horse, with a negro page carrying his helmet. The tapestry on the lower flight depicts Charles II, again bareheaded, in armour, riding a bay. In the left foreground is Mars driving away a dragon, with Mercury in the centre and the old City of London in the background.

All four designs were copied from Abraham van Diepenbeeck's illustrations for the duke's famous book on horsemanship, first published in Antwerp in 1658.

THE YELLOW DRAWING ROOM

This room was a library from 1822 to 1927, when it became a breakfast room. Boudin produced the present design for a drawing room in 1936, silk damask replacing grey oak panelling and the windows being lowered to the floor. Before the war it was used as a luncheon room, becoming a drawing room after 1945. Above the fine Palladian chimneypiece based on a design by Inigo Jones is *The Pulcinello's Kitchen* by Giovanni Domenico Tiepolo the younger (1727–1804), whose Pulcinello fresco cycle is now in the Museo del Settecento Veneziano (Ca' Rezzonico) on the Grand Canal in Venice. The fine Chinese porcelain includes two blue and white lamps from the reign of Emperor Kangxi (1662–1722), and a pair of *famille rose* hawks and garniture of five ruby ground *famille rose* vases from the reign of Qianlong (1736–95). Above the ebonised and brass ornamental William IV bookcases hangs a pair of flower paintings by Jean-Baptiste Monnoyer (1634–99), who executed many flowerpieces for the 1st Duke of Montagu after 1677, most of which are now at Boughton House, Northamptonshire. On the floor is a copy of Lady Baillie's original mid-eighteenth-century carpet, said to have been made by monks at a St Petersburg monastery. The furniture is chiefly English, dating from the late seventeenth and early eighteenth centuries, and the enamelled gilt French *verre églomisé* looking glass was made around 1700.

THE THORPE HALL ROOM

This room is an outstanding example of English mid-seventeenth-century decorative art. The marble chimneypiece and the wood panelling were acquired for Lady Baillie in 1927 by Sir Charles Allom, of White Allom, from the principal room at Thorpe Hall near Peterborough, designed in 1653 by Peter Mills for Chief Justice Oliver St John. With Sir Christopher Wren, Mills was one of the architects commissioned to supervise the rebuilding of London after the Great Fire of 1666. The panelling was stripped of old green paint to the pine beneath after installation at Leeds.

Complementing the classical chimneypiece superbly, the black marble bust of a youth is Italian and dates from about 1700. The furniture is also mostly of the eighteenth century, with fine examples of both English and French workmanship. There are two Louis XV armchairs, and a twelve-fold Kangxi early-eighteenth-century coromandel screen.

The bird-life that features everywhere at Leeds is also found here in the collection of eighteenth- and early nineteenth-century Chinese porcelain.

A Qianlong famille rose *phoenix with harlequin plumage, perched on rockwork, mid to late eighteenth century.*

THE INNER HALL AND THE FRONT HALL

The entrance hall to the main part of the castle situated at the north end of the island has undergone radical change in modern times. From 1822 to 1926 the area between the stairwell wall and the window over-looking the bailey was a small drawing room. When he remodelled the hall in 1927, the French designer Rateau pierced the wall with three Gothic arches leading to the staircase.

In the inner hall at either side of the Thorpe Hall Room doorway, and on the wall opposite these hang three Flemish *feuilles de choux* tapestries, from either Enghien or Grammont, mid-sixteenth-century. The large Nuremberg iron bound chest under the window is early seven-teenth-century, and on the window sill is an Austrian or North Italian comedy figure.

In the front hall the mid-seventeenth-century oak and walnut six-legged refectory table has carved on it the date AD 16 and 39. Three medieval swords and one German sixteenth-century broadsword hang on the walls, in addition to Van Dyck's portrait of Prince Charles Louis KG (1618–80), Elector Palatine of the Rhine, nephew of Charles I and elder brother of Prince Rupert, the celebrated Royalist Commander.

One of the small windows in the front hall giving onto the bailey.

Detail from one of the sixteenth-century Flemish tapestries hanging in the hall.

Portrait possibly of Mr Francis Brand, Gentleman
of the Privy Chamber, his dog's collars inscribed
'Hampton Court March 7 1671' and 'Hampton Court
May 6 1671'. Painted by Lenthall, once owned
by the Bowyer Smith baronets.

German portrait of dogs belonging to an English
officer, c.1800.

1

2

3

4

5

THE GATE TOWER AND DOG COLLAR MUSEUM

The Gate Tower (see page 9) contains, to the east, rooms for entertaining in the former guard room and stables, and on the first floor where the Constable's rooms were situated, the curator's office. On the western side is the Dog Collar Museum.

Dogs have always been present at Leeds Castle throughout the ages – hounds for hunting, gundogs, mastiffs to guard the Castle gates, spaniels and lapdogs to grace the apartments of widowed queens. Lady Baillie was never without several dogs, and it is only fitting that Leeds should now house such a fine collection of antique dog collars. The collection which ranges over four hundred years, was generously presented to the Leeds Castle Foundation by Mrs Gertrude Hunt in memory of her husband John Hunt, the distinguished Irish scholar. The collection has been extended by gifts from private owners and by the Foundation's acquisitions.

A separate guidebook to the collars is on sale to visitors.

1 French bronze collar, c.1800.

2 Collars for Lord Talbot's winners of the Great Champion Puppy Stakes for All England, 1838.

3 German iron and brass hinged collar, first half of eighteenth century.

4 Italian brass collar, c.1630–50, the pierced and chased acanthus work engraved with the owner's arms.

5 Mid-eighteenth-century Austrian leather collar with the arms of its owner.

The Culpeper Garden, Aviary, Maze and Grotto, Greenhouses and Vineyard

THE STABLE YARD AND FAIRFAX HALL

THE CULPEPER GARDEN

Leaving the castle precincts visitors pass along a causeway to the Stable Yard and the Fairfax Hall, between the Moat and the Great Water, an extra defence which could be filled in times of danger and now adds to the natural beauty of the park. When country estates were entirely self-supporting barns were an important element in the farm economy. Dating in part from as early as 1680 the barn, now called the Fairfax Hall to recall that family, was restored in 1822–23 and since 1975 has been adapted into an attractive restaurant. Within the barn annex are articles associated with previous owners of Leeds. At one period Lady Baillie's sister, the Hon. Dorothy Paget, the well known racehorse owner and breeder, stabled some of her horses here, and the clock above the archway came from Epsom racecourse. Buildings surrounding the yard have been put to good use by the Foundation, providing residential conference accommodation, shops and catering.

The Culpeper Garden was created in 1980 by Russell Page, the international garden designer, on an oddly-shaped sloping plot of land which for hundreds of years had served as the kitchen garden. It is named after the Culpeper family, owners of Leeds in the seventeenth century.

The garden is enclosed on three sides by the warm brick of old estate buildings and a high wall, while the remaining side looks out over the Great Water. The flower beds, edged with low box hedges, are arranged in an informal pattern and separated by brick and grass pathways, so that visitors have the impression of walking through a field of flowers. The flowers themselves are those of an old English cottage garden – roses, pinks, lad's love and lavender, poppies and lupins – but with some more exotic blooms mingled among the old favourites, and many with wonderful scents.

The garden is also home to the national collections of catmint and bergamot – grown here under the guidance of the National Council for the Conservation of Plants and Gardens, based at Wisley Gardens, Surrey.

As a final touch, a herb border has been planted along the old wall, something which might have pleased the famous seventeenth-century herbalist, Nicholas Culpeper, a distant kinsman of the family that lived at Leeds.

Van der Decken's Hornbill
(Tockus deckeni)

Toco Toucan
(Ramphastos toco)

Kookaburra
(Dacelo novae-guineae)

THE AVIARY

The first aviaries at Leeds Castle were established in the late 1950s to house Lady Baillie's collection of small Australian finches. Over the years her enthusiasm brought many rare and varied species to the Castle and she developed a special interest in parakeets, particularly the Australian and Ringneck varieties.

The new Aviary, bearing the name of Lady Baillie at its entrance, was opened in 1988 by Princess Alexandra, Royal Patron of the Leeds Castle Foundation. Designed by the architect Vernon Gibberd, of London, it incorporates the most progressive ideas of modern aviculture. The twin aims of the collection of over one hundred species are the fostering of public awareness of the importance of wildlife conservation, and breeding with a view to the reintroduction of captive-bred young and endangered species into their original habitats.

A separate guide on the Aviary is on sale to visitors.

Palm Cockatoo (Probosciger aterrimus)

Swainson's Lorikeet (Trichoglossus haematodus)

THE MAZE AND GROTTO

The Maze, designed by the architect Vernon Gibberd in association with Minotaur Designs, was planted in 1988 with 2,400 yew trees. When mature, it will present the appearance of a topiary castle with castellated hedges forming towers and bastions. At the centre is a mound, with a spiralling path leading up to a raised viewpoint affording a panoramic view of the Park and surrounding countryside, a feature in the eighteenth-century tradition for the purpose of 'viewing the estate'. From this vantage point, the perceptive visitor will discern in the Maze's plan a queen's crown, echoing 'the Castle of the Queens of England'.

Mazes or labyrinths have developed from an ancient Egyptian building near Lake Maeris which contained twelve courts and 3,000 chambers. During the Middle Ages a Maze or Labyrinth was frequently indicated on the floors of French cathedrals. In gardening the Maze is a remnant of the old geometrical style of planting.

The mound is in fact a hollow dome containing the entrance to the Grotto from the Maze, so that the task of unravelling the return route is replaced by an exciting and unexpected alternative return journey. The Grotto, designed by Vernon Gibberd with the collaboration of the sculptor Simon Verity and the shell artist Diana Reynell, takes the visitor from the light of day into the Underworld, and through fantastic vicissitudes back to the real world again.

At the entrance to the grotto are Simon Verity's *Guardians of the Sources of Water*. Steps lead down past a pattern of coloured stones whose inspiration derives from the tapestries in the Castle. In the main chamber the *Four Elements*, by Diana Reynell, guarded by mythical beasts, stand in niches. The coffered ceiling is decorated with swans, symbols of alchemy and a characteristic of Leeds Castle. As the visitor descends, design themes become more macabre. Bones emerge from the walls like fossils. Fish fly on the ceiling and creatures walk upside down. The walls are encrusted with exotic minerals.

At the tunnel exit the mood lightens with a shell Phoenix, representing rebirth, in its secret guarded cave. Roots protrude as if from mammoth forest trees above. Daylight finally enters the tunnel and the visitor emerges into a square hermitage formed by the retaining walls of the end steps and roofed by the bridge leading to the Maze entrance above.

Leeds Castle maze

Grotto figures in the chambers of the Styx.

The giant Typhoeus, father of the Harpies, tried to overpower the gods but was vanquished by Zeus and placed under Mount Etna, where he became the source of fire. Here Typhoeus struggles against the weight of the mountain, lava flowing from his mouth. The dome is decorated with black and white swans, symbols of alchemy and of Leeds Castle.

THE GREENHOUSES AND VINEYARD

On his first visit to Virginia in the 1730s, Lord Fairfax collected plants which he sent home to the hothouses at Leeds; they included chinquapin, wild olive, ginseng and indigo roots. In return he sent apple trees from Kent to Virginia and the area of the Shenandoah Valley, where his house Greenway Court was situated, is still famed for apple growing. Nowadays not only fuchsias and other colourful blooms are grown in the greenhouses for the exclusive decoration of the house, but also peaches and nectarines for the Castle table. Plants and flowers grown at Leeds may be purchased at the greenhouses.

One of two vineyards in Kent recorded in the Domesday Book in 1086, the same site is being cultivated again after a five-century lapse. Leeds Castle now makes wine from a blend of Müller Thurgau and Seyval Blanc grapes, which is sold in the restaurant and shops under its own label.

MEDIUM DRY 1992 · LEEDS·CASTLE·MAIDSTONE·KENT · WHITE WINE 1992

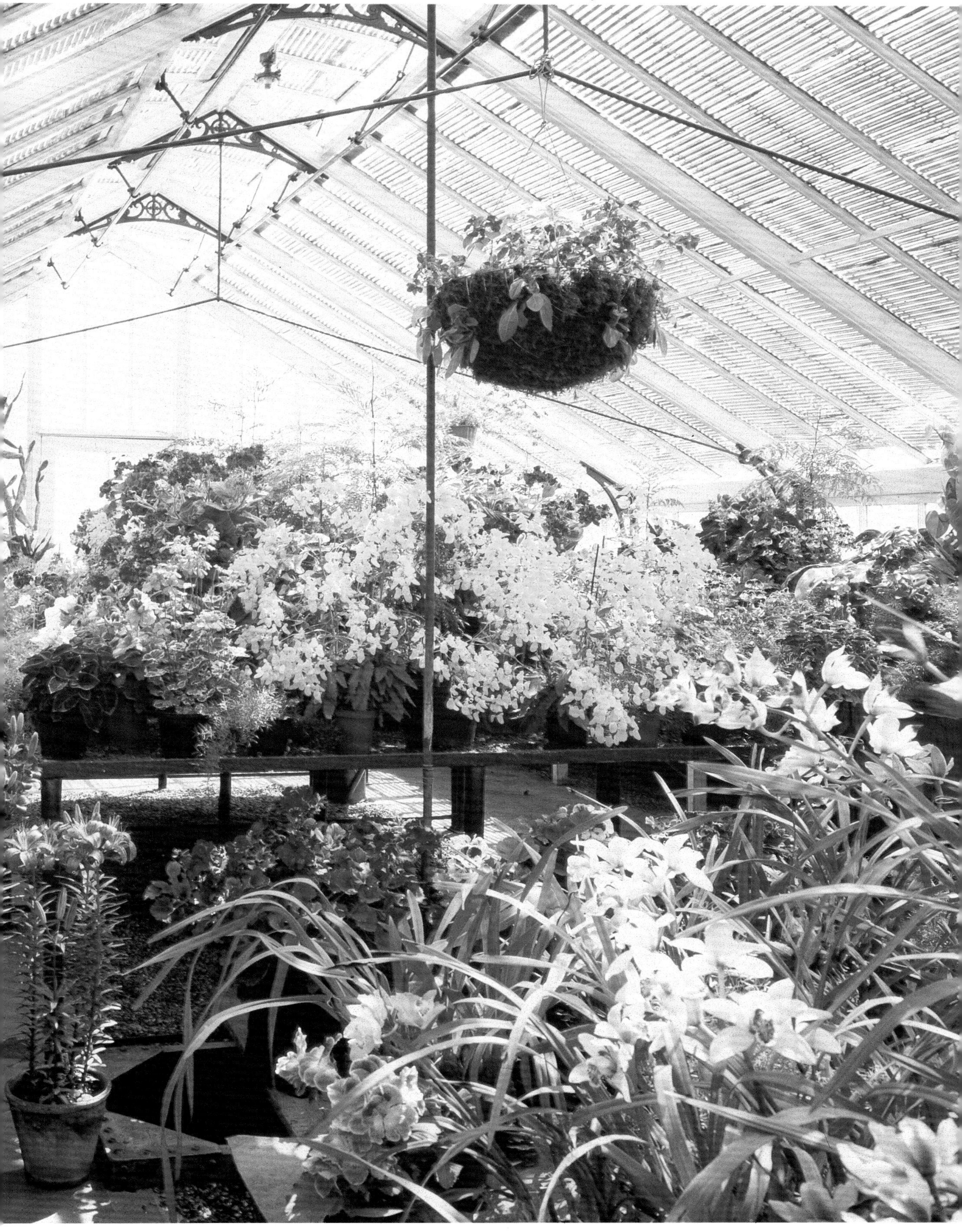

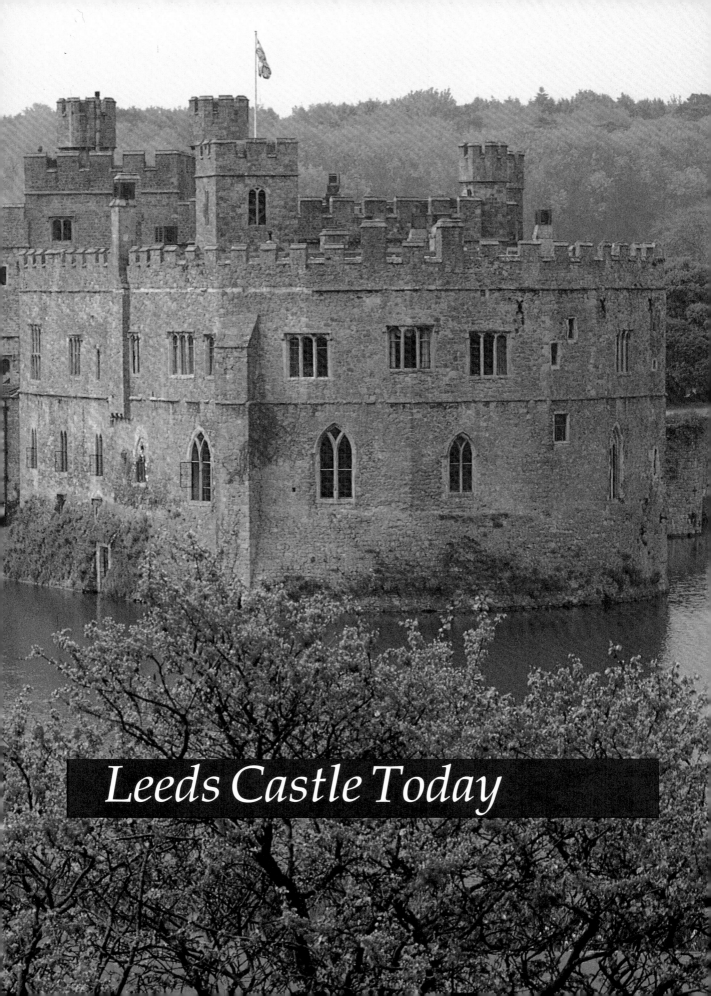

Leeds Castle Today

Leeds Castle was bought by the Hon. Mrs Wilson Filmer, Lady Baillie as she became, in 1926, when she was only twenty-six years of age. In the succeeding years she restored it with meticulous care, and in the last years of her life she devoted much energy to finding a means whereby the Castle could be preserved as a living castle, without becoming what she called a stone museum, and without the need for Government support.

She decided that her purposes would best be achieved by the establishment of a charity formed specifically for the purpose of preserving Leeds Castle in perpetuity for the benefit and enjoyment of the public. The charity would also have wider duties, if funds permitted, to promote certain other charitable activities including the use of the Castle for significant national and international medical seminars and for artistic and cultural events. Lady Baillie hoped that the Castle could also be used for important meetings of international statesmen. In addition she provided powers for the Castle and its park to be used for conferences and other activities which would earn the money required to maintain the Castle, its parkland and their amenities, and to fulfil the other purposes of the charity.

The charity so established is known as the Leeds Castle Foundation, to which were transferred the Castle, its contents and its parkland, together with an endowment which would help to meet the costs of carrying out the purposes of the charity.

The Trustees of the Foundation, which receives no Government support and (unlike the National Trust) no support from subscriptions and legacies, seek so to manage Leeds Castle and the resources and activities associated with it as to enable them to give effect to Lady Baillie's wish to see the Castle and its parkland preserved for public benefit and enjoyment, while protecting its unique character and quality as a historic house in a tranquil and beautiful setting. The Trustees of the Leeds Castle Foundation are: *Patron*: Her Royal Highness Princess Alexandra GCVO, the Honourable Lady Ogilvy. *Chairman*: The Right Honourable Lord Thomson of Monifieth KT DL; the Honourable Edward Adeane CVO; the Lord Armstrong of Ilminster GCB CVO; Sir Roger Bannister CBE DM FRCP; the Lord Boston of Faversham QC; the Right Honourable Lord Charteris of Amisfield GCB GCVO QSO OBE; Dame Elizabeth Esteve-Coll DBE; Monsieur Gerald Van der Kemp, Membre de L'Institut (France); the Right Honourable Lord Kingsdown KG; Peter Mimpriss Esq; the Honourable Sir Angus Ogilvy KCVO; the Earl of Scarbrough; Dr John Stokes MD FRCP; James Teacher Esq; Sir John Ure KCMG LVO.

THE PRIVATE ROOMS

These rooms are used for important conferences and other meetings and are not open to the public.

Designed by Stéphane Boudin in 1936, the Dining Room is a clever blending of French and English styles. Five Louis XVI Aubusson pastoral tapestries, *c.*1780, are set in panels and at each end of the room are displayed pieces from Lady Baillie's collection of Chinese porcelain.

Since its construction in 1822 the Library has had several uses. Until 1926 it served as a small dining room. Lady Baillie used it first as a schoolroom where her daughters received their early education. In 1936 Stéphane Boudin redesigned it after a late seventeenth-century model by Daniel Marot (1663–1752), who worked for the Duke of Buccleugh at Boughton House. Marot was a French Huguenot refugee, who fled to the Court of William of Orange in 1684. The portrait of a young boy with a falcon above the chimneypiece is of the circle of Jacob Cuyp (born 1575).

The Cream Room is the only bedroom that retains the original panelling of 1822. The bed is surmounted by a half tester covered in ivory silk with eighteenth-century floral embroidery. The paintings include flower pictures by Pierre Redouté (1759–1840) and bird pictures by Christoph Ludwig Agricola (1677–1719).

The Board Room

The Cream Room, one of twenty bedrooms – four in the Gloriette and the rest in the main Castle – available to those attending conferences at Leeds Castle.

The Dining Room

The Library

SPECIAL OCCASIONS

True to its historical tradition as a royal castle, Leeds has been visited on many occasions by HRH Princess Alexandra, Royal Patron of the Leeds Castle Foundation. Her Majesty The Queen visited the Castle in 1981.

Throughout the year Leeds Castle plays host to a number of Special Events. Annual Events include a New Year's Day treasure trail, an Easter egg hunt in the Castle grounds, a festival of English wine in May, a balloon fiesta in June, open-air concerts in June and July and a grand firework display in November. Special concerts also take place, such as Luciano Pavarotti's in August 1993.

Disabled visitors have always been welcome at Leeds, and they were present on the occasion of Her Majesty the Queen's visit in 1981.

HRH Princess Alexandra visiting the Castle on 25 May 1988 with her husband, Sir Angus Ogilvy, listens to the address of welcome by the second Chairman of the Foundation, Lord Aldington.

Leeds Castle in November

LEEDS CASTLE TODAY

During the Flower Festival in September, the interior of the Castle is decorated throughout with flowers, fruit and vegetables.

The 1812 Overture being performed, with fireworks and cannon of the Royal Artillery, at an open-air concert of popular classics.

Leeds Castle's nine-hole golf-course built as a private course in 1930, in the magnificent surroundings of the Park, is open to the public. It was reconstructed in 1988.

Luciano Pavarotti at Leeds Castle, August 1993.

At the International Balloon and Vintage Car Fiesta, the racing balloons are chased by vintage cars.

Acknowledgements

The publishers are grateful to the following people for their contributions to the text:

David Cleggett
Jonathan Keates
The late Lord Geoffrey-Lloyd
The late Peter Wilson, CBE
Vernon Gibberd
Minotaur Designs

The photographs were taken by Angelo Hornak, with the exception of the following:

John Vere Brown pp.40 (*above*), 40-41, 42, 43
Nick Daley p.70 (*left*)
Barry Duffield pp.6-7
Adrian Fisher/Minotaur p.68
Paul Hillman pp.10, 18, 23, 24, 62 (*second and third from left*)
David Hosking pp.32 (*Shelduck, Ringed Teal*), 67
David Noble p.77 (*right*)
Mike Shield p.79
Sloman and Pettitt p.76 (*left, both*)
Ronald White p.18 (*top*)
Andy Williams pp.62-63, 65, 70-71

For permission to reproduce illustrations the publishers are grateful to the following:

The Lady Anne Bentinck pp.52-53
The British Library p.40 (*below*)
Interiors Magazine pp.40 (*above*), 41, 42-43
Kent County Archives pp.20-21
The Curator, Maidstone Museum and Art Gallery pp.10, 24
National Geographic Society p.79
Philip Wykeham Martin p.23

The painting on pp.16-17 is in a private collection, and we are most grateful to the owners, Col. and Mrs Remington-Hobbs, for allowing us to reproduce it.

The maps on pp.36-37 and on the back cover were devised and painted by Terence Dalley.

A fourteenth-century iron key recovered from the mud near the Gate Tower when the moat was cleaned in 1823.